WOODWORKING MASTERY

The Complete Step By Step Project
Guide to Furniture Making
Techniques and Skills

STEVE CHARLES

Table of Contents

CHAPTER ONE 2

   INTRODUCTION 2

CHAPTER TWO 6

   DIY PROJECTS ON WOODMAKING OR
FURNITURE MAKING 6

CHAPTER THREE 21

   SHOE ORGANIZER OR ARRANGER 21

CHAPTER FOUR 30

   OPEN AIR TABLE 30

CHAPTER FIVE 37

   FURNITURE FINISH GUIDE 37

THE END 39

CHAPTER ONE

INTRODUCTION

WOODWORKING OR FURNITURE PROJECTS

Carpentry or furniture making is an interest that can look rather overwhelming; studying the instrument plans conceivable on explicit records make you wonder how you can ever discover the space or bear the cost of the devices. In any case, there are two or three immediate and simple to do accommodating assignments that you can make at home that can be advantageously worked in a little open space and with only a few mechanical gatherings.

In all honesty, different skilled experts esteem finding accommodating carpentry extends that can be made utilizing only a couple of gadgets. In the event that your space is essentially nothing, pay extraordinary brain to undertakings that offer furthermore putting away choices, for example, little rack units. Other satisfying undertakings intertwine limit boxes that can serve both, as a side table, and as an ensured about storing up for difficult to reach garments or covers.

"There are different essential and viable carpentry sets out to do at home that can be enough worked in to some degree open space."The Beauty of Woodworking

Making sense of how to work with wood causes you develop your basic reasoning aptitudes, increase your logical mastery, and manufacture your ability to imagine. On the off chance that you're trying to get the hang of carpentry in a limited space, you can in like manner develop your ability to think in an immediate way and genuinely collect your masterminding capacities.

Carpentry requires focus, and that can be slippery in our forefront, hyper-related world. Your woodshop can be a spot freed from electronic contraptions, or if nothing else a spot where you desert your cell phone. The path toward working with your hands, distributing an endeavor and assembling your work impacts the psyche in habits that simply watching chronicles or regardless, amassing in a book can't.

Carpentry will allow you be an understudy. Learning new aptitudes is a mind blowing technique to sustain your sentiment of order over your life and assembling your boldness or reliance.

In like manner, a basic level of physical wellbeing is imperative to furniture making or woodwork. If all else fails, this activity anticipates that you should stand, bend, lift and distort. In case your regular work remembers contributing a huge amount of vitality for a seat, this hobby can help bolster your body similarly as your cerebrum.

CHAPTER TWO

DIY PROJECTS ON WOODMAKING OR FURNITURE MAKING

Locally built Wine Glass Holder

This wine glass holder is an exceptional badge of the greatness that can be found in little family unit things or wood. To complete this endeavor adequately, you need a touch of wood 7.5 inches square. Guarantee that if there are any packs, they're not in the board or at any of the corners.

A pack in a touch of wood centers to a zone of the living tree where a branch kicked the basin and tumbled off. Notwithstanding the way that bundles could be stunning, realize that the wood around a pack and inside the bundle will be an altogether unexpected surface in comparison to the wood around it; it may be all the more eagerly to expel and may fall as you work around it.

The model for the wine glass holder is really clear. The hole in the board fits over the container top, and the openings in the corner hold the wine glass stems. You may find that you'll give indications of progress fit if you fix within opening to flare down over the wine bottle so it doesn't wobble.

In any case you finally decide to design this, you'll end up with a supportive bit of craftwork that would make an ideal present or gift!

Locally built Birdhouses

Roost rooms are splendidly useful little errands that anticipate that you should enter a straight hole and amass a tough joint where two bits of wood get together. Our model aviaries feature, not simply recolored fence wood for extensive stretches of organization, yet furthermore shingles!

These aviaries are amassed with a brad nailer and close by weapon. When working with both of these mechanical assemblies, it's basic to work with snaps and straight edges. A metal square is an exceptional gadget for setting up a 90-degree point, yet it may not be a clasp.

DIY Headboard and Bed Frame

In case you have a futon yet need a bed, this versatile DIY adventure will permit you to play with stroll, upholstery foam, quilt batting and stain for the base. Paint can in like manner be used on your bed layout, so have some great occasions. This endeavor is definitely not hard to grow, on and on versatile and will go with no issue.

This is exceptional contrasted with other locally built furniture adventures for kids with increasingly prepared age run. Not only would they have the option to contribute some vitality getting some answers concerning contraption security and real dealing with, yet they can alter the endeavor and having something expected to their tendency and worked without any other individual.

On the off chance that it's not all that much difficulty note that this endeavor fuses shower foam concrete, which may viably blast bursts or into flares. Work this assignment with a great deal of ventilation and avoid using this endeavor near fire, for instance, your radiator.

Rack

A best time viewpoint in regards to working with wood is that you can work with things recently fabricated, or disassemble existing things to make various things. The layered nursery rack features fragmented CD cases from the rough woods territory of a standard make shop.

The cases are flipped onto their backs to fill in as a plant pot holding plate, and wooden furniture feet, pre-handled, are added to the base. Finally, the space between the racks is versatile and can be changed depending upon the length of your dowels.

This is another assignment with a great deal of systems built straightforwardly in. If you choose to use this speak to taking care of anything particularly overpowering, or if children will use it, consider mounting the dowels in spines that you can screw to the container for an unrivaled and an undeniably consistent view.

Outside X Table

This brilliant outdoors X table can offer the sum of the strikingly versatile characteristics of wood. It will in general be made with additional fence sheets, and it might be made sense of so you can design it to fit with the materials you have.

The table in the model is worked with materials proper to the outside, yet you can manufacture yours to work inside your home. Choose the proportion of wood you have and to allow you plan appropriately. The configuration for the x-underpins on which the table stands was a direct square state of scrap stagger; you could use cardboard if that is what you have.

At the point when the x-bolster was spread out, the point cuts for the top and base of the legs were settled, stepped and cut. If you have a miter saw, you can use that, yet this plan on scrap infers you don't

need to put aside the push to understand the edges.

Wooden Wine Rack

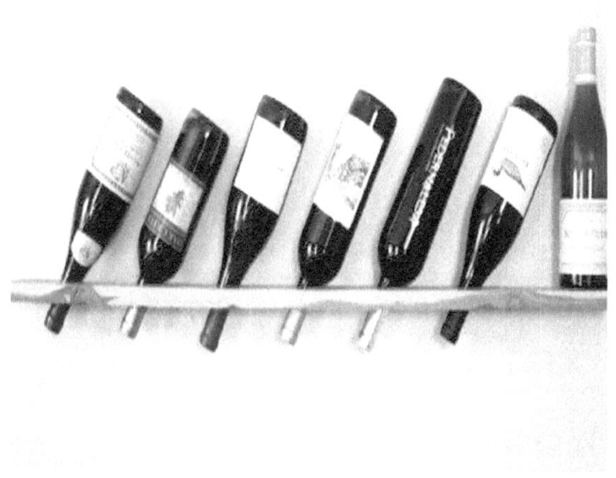

This thinks about visual area of some proportion of wood, for instance, an oak floor or pine table top, is stunning. Regardless, a singular piece of stand-out wood, for instance, cedar, hickory or tiger maple, can be captivating.

This wood board wine rack is genuinely not an incredibly speedy endeavor. While it may be worked with hand instruments, you should develop a mechanical assembly to hold the board while you drill the openings at the right edge.

Realize that the bearings don't offer much to the extent hanging your wine rack. Consider placing assets into decorating areas to mount underneath; when stacked, this board may be incredibly overpowering.

Workbench For Sparing Space

This direct yet amazingly supportive wrinkle down workbench could work in a lot of employments. In the event that you're basically starting and don't have the advantages for a kitchen table, this solid divider mounted table could work well for somewhat family very. This table could in like manner fill in as a claim to fame workspace or sideboard if space is compelled.

It takes a lump gateway or squeezed wood, two lengths of metal pipe with ribs, a 2x4 as long as the portals, and some generous turns. Choose the height you need and cut the channels to length. Mount the 2x4 to the divider at the right height to organize the metal channels.

With your drill, screw the turns to the opposite side of the door and the channel ribs to the uttermost corners of the passage. Screw the channels into the spines to get to a suitable working height, and get some help or some supporting; you'll need to crawl under your table to join the turns to the 2 x 4. At the point when you're set, clear the channels and cover the table down.

CHAPTER THREE

SHOE ORGANIZER OR ARRANGER

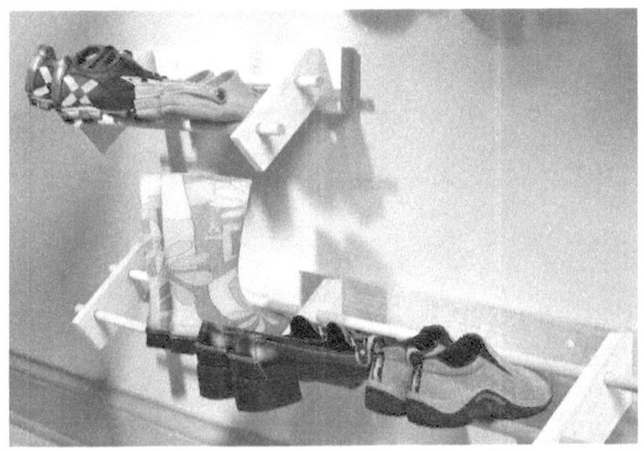

In case you plan doing a straightforward wood adventures for kids, this is an ideal task. It's versatile, will fit in a wide scope of regions, and incorporates only a dash of cutting and a couple of dowels. Also, the kids get the chance to deal with finding divider studs!

This shoe organizer starts with two backings cut from your 1 x 4, with holes drilled per the model for the dowels. Mount the backings to your 1 x 3, run the dowels through the holes and screw or nail them set up.

It's noteworthy not to go unnecessarily wide. In case you can find dowels longer than 48 inches and need to put in a long shoe rack, put in extra backings to swear off bowing the dowel after some time.

Magazine Storage Bins

Scanning for carpentry expands that sell? Limit is reliably notable, and these essential magazine racks would be well known among scrapbookers and other strength fans.

The materials list for these magazine holders is exceptionally short; you need 1/4 pine and 1/4" compacted wood. Birch compacted wood or 1/4" mahogany would finish enjoyably. To cut the twists, you need a 5-gallon compartment for a configuration.

Luckily, you can tape the packed wood together to cut the curves. Work progressively and let your jigsaw complete the obligation. Your 1 x 4 will concur with the edges of the squeezed wood and you can nail the box alongside a brad nailer.

You will require a drill to make a "pull opening" in the front of the container. At the point when you've cut your 1 x 4 into bits of the right length, you can quickly stamp all of the four of these openings and drill them consistently.

Outside Wooden Bench

Scanning for woodshop adventures for auxiliary school understudies? This seat will decidedly serve. It's created from two 10' long 2 x 8 bits of atmosphere safe wood. Since people will be roosted on this, keep away from anything that's slanted to dividing.

This wooden seat is stacked with captivating edges. You'll moreover require a countersink bore. An indirect saw will take care of business to cut through the 2 x 8s. In this event, a jigsaw would be hard pressed.

You will require a drill and 2-1/2" deck screws. Luckily, these screws are totally indulgent and may be staggering practice for a drill novice.

Sliding Bookend

If you are courageous bits of old or especially pretty hardwood, these sliding bookends show how little carpentry musings can go to strikingly exquisite endeavors.

These bookends incorporate a slim space and fit really over the standard body of the rack to shape a comfortable square against the largeness of near to books. This endeavor would be great done up in cherry, maple or oak. If you get the choice to develop the racks similarly as the bookends, you could upgrade this rack with a combination of hardwood bookends and prepare a magnificent, stand-apart family thing.

Direct Storage Box

For those of us who use woodshop adventure contemplations as an average motivation to go mechanical assembly shopping, you're in karma! The essential accumulating box featured here requires a scone joiner. This instrument isn't an excess; it makes it possible to join sheets into stages. You'll have to play with this for quite a while in the occasion that you've never used one to guarantee you get the cuts in the right spot or your sheets will have an edge.

A deliberately collected limit seat offers a great deal of flexibility. You can use this as an end table, a side table or a youth's playbox. Make certain to present moderate close rotates if kids will play around this seat.

CHAPTER FOUR

OPEN AIR TABLE

This is one of the most supportive DIY wood furniture adventures you'll find. While the impression of this open air table is greater than that of one with the seats joined with the table, you'll have fundamentally more space to move around with this structure.

Your outside table will be grown through and through of 2 x 4's, so you understand it will last. Another strategy for certain customers, a dado joint, ought to be cut into the x-propping of the legs. The table legs and seat legs all fit in a comparative trough, estimated for the dainty edge of the 2 x 4.

The dado joint expels wood from each piece of lumber that shapes the x that supports the table. At the point when you realize how much wood ought to be cleared, you can use a switch or an engraving to play out this task.

Wooden Cutting Board

If none of your carpentry adventures get money and you'd like to change that, building custom cutting sheets may be a way to deal with improve your salary. These instruments can be created utilizing small amounts of wood, intentionally joined to various bits of wood, so each will be uncommon and changed to the buyer. Without a doubt, even little bits of wood can be used in a custom cutting board. A bit of cutting barricade can end being useful in an outdoors continuance pack. You can similarly consolidate it with a better than average cheddar sharp edge for a mind blowing woman favoring. The potential results are inconceivable!

This video incorporates a table saw. While the ace on the video underneath doesn't use a security watch, youngster carpentry gadgets should never be used with the prosperity ousted. Table saws cut whatever you put before them. Work your wood wide enough that the prosperity watch stays on until you have a great deal of comprehension added to your collection.

Locally built Picture Frames

Locally developed picture traces offer decorators the chance to put custom bits of workmanship, glass or surface endeavors into an exceptionally fitted packaging for gloriousness and joy. These are mind boggling wood adventures for fledglings and can be worked with a miter saw set at 45 degrees, or a table saw with a 45-degree move.

Custom picture housings can be delivered utilizing new wood or old edges, and gigantic edges can be slashed down for stand-out things. On the off chance that you're looking for little carpentry expands that you can play with to build up your saw capacities, custom picture plots are an ideal dare to start on!

Normal Edge Lazy Susan

Woodworkers of all stripes will like this assignment! You start with a cutting contraption, work with processors of a couple of sizes, ultimately wrap up with a dressmaker's iron!

For the prosperity of security, hit a reused shop and get an iron for your shop. Do whatever it takes not to strike the storeroom for this gadget; the paste used in the glow activated wood tape is strong and tenacious. Make an effort not to get that stick on the nuclear family iron.

As showed up in the video underneath, the trademark edge lazy susan is a striking piece that will be a magnificent grandstand for party food on an open air table. This piece will credit itself impeccably to any regular elaborate format or solid food appear. Dazzling!

CHAPTER FIVE

FURNITURE FINISH GUIDE

Your wood adventures musings will really sparkle in the keep going application in case they get an exceptional fulfillment. OK prefer to recolor the piece, or leave it typical? Is it exact to state that you are foreseeing water or oil based consummation?

In the going with video, ace Colin Knecht proposes testing the sogginess in your carpentry shop before you start finishing; if the wetness is unnecessarily high, the wood may develop and the culmination will dry too step by step. If your shop is especially vulnerable against the segments, you may truly need to check the atmosphere before applying the fruition. It's in like manner a shrewd idea to check the grain with a bit of scouring alcohol; if the wood muddies up, it needs increasingly fine sanding.

Your end-use is fundamental in picking a fulfillment. Various basic little wood adventures, for instance, cutting sheets, need a food-safe consummation.

In case you are set up to start creating your woodshop, by then this fun and beneficial recreation movement will bring you unbelievable fulfillment. Wood is responsive and unendingly supportive, and once you OK with a model or strategy, you can adjust it to suit the necessities of your space. From side tables to limit racks, wine racks to open air tables, this redirection will add to your own fulfillment.

THE END